WORLD OF

MAMMALS

RHINOS

by Peter Murray

Content Adviser: Barbara E. Brown, Associate, Mammal Division, The Field Museum, Chicago, IL

THE CHILD'S WORLD®, CHANHASSEN, MINNESOTA

The Child's World

RHINOS

Published in the United States of America by The Child's World®
PO Box 326 • Chanhassen, MN 55317-0326 • 800-599-READ • www.childsworld.com

Acknowledgements:

The Child's World®: Mary Berendes, Publishing Director

Editorial Directions, Inc.: E. Russell Primm, Editorial Director; Pam Rosenberg, Editor;
Judith Shiffer, Assistant Editor; Matt Messbarger, Editorial Assistant; Susan Hindman,
Copy Editor; Emily Dolbear, Proofreader; Judith Frisbie and Olivia Nellums, Fact
Checkers; Tim Griffin/IndexServ, Indexer; Cian Loughlin O'Day, Photo Researcher, Linda
S. Koutris, Photo Editor

The Design Lab: Kathleen Petelinsek, Designer, Production Artist, and Cartographer

Photos:

Cover: Corbis; half title/CIP: Getty Images/Photodisc; frontispiece: Paul A. Souders/
Corbis.

Interior: Animals Animals/Earth Scenes: 8 (ABPL/Clem Haagner), 16 (Trevor Barrett),
29 (Khalid Ghani); Corbis: 5-top left, 5-top right and 13 (Archivo Iconografico, S.A.), 11
(Peter Johnson), 19 (Martin Harvey), 20 (Terry Whittaker), Frank Lane Picture Agency),
25 (Heinrich van den Berg); Digital Vision: 5-bottom right and 32, 5-bottom left and 36;
Getty Images/Taxi: 23 (Peter Lilja), 31 (Wendy Dennis); Getty Images/Photodisc/James
Gritz: 5-middle left and 26; Photodisc: 15, 34.

Library of Congress Cataloging-in-Publication Data

Murray, Peter, 1952 Sept. 29–
  Rhinos / by Peter Murray.
    p. cm. — (The world of mammals)
  Includes index.
  ISBN 1-59296-502-4 (lib. bdg. : alk. paper) 1. Rhinoceroses—Juvenile literature. I. Title.
II. World of mammals (Chanhassen, Minn.)
  QL737.U63M87 2005
  599.66'8—dc22   2005000534

TABLE OF CON

Chapter One

Endangered Giants

It is early morning in Tanzania, Africa. As the sun rises over Ngorongoro Crater, the vast Serengeti Plain comes to life. Herds of zebras move through the grasslands. A giraffe stretches its long neck to nibble tender leaves from an acacia tree. Leopards lie in wait beside **game trails.** Monkeys chatter from the treetops.

At the edge of a patch of forest, an African black rhinoceros (*Diceros bicornis*) rises slowly to her feet, blinking in the morning light. She raises her horned snout and sniffs the breeze. She rotates her large, scoop-shaped ears, listening for sounds of danger.

The female rhino weighs about 1,300 kilograms (2,860 pounds), her skin is thick and tough, and she has two long, sharp horns jutting from her nose and forehead. What is she afraid of? Adult rhinos are safe from lions, hyenas, and other natural **predators.** What could threaten such a huge creature?

The rhino makes a high-pitched noise that sounds like a cat mewing. She starts to walk from the protection

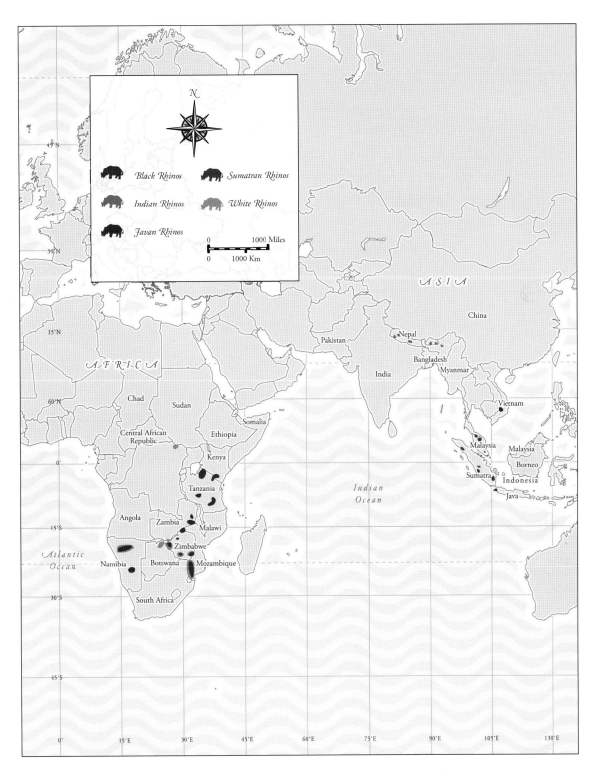

Africa and Asia are home to the world's dwindling population of rhinos.

7

of the trees out onto the grassland. Behind her, a small rhino calf struggles to its feet and runs to catch up to her. The calf is only a few days old. It looks like a smaller version of its mother but without the horns.

The mother rhino stops to nibble some leaves from a bush. The baby rhino nuzzles her side, hoping for milk.

A black rhino calf stays close to its mother. Baby rhinos, like many other young animals, are in constant danger of being killed by predators.

Weighing only about 50 kilograms (110 lbs), the calf is in constant danger from predators. Only by staying close to its mother can it hope to survive.

About 1,000 kilometers (622 miles) to the south, on the grassy plains of South Africa, eight white rhinos **graze.** The white rhino (*Ceratotherium simum*) is one of the largest land animals on Earth.

The white rhinos spend much of the day eating, clipping the grass short with their wide mouths. White rhinos are carefully protected by the South African government. This slow-moving herd has little to fear.

Its heavy skin dotted with knobby bumps and hanging in thick folds, the Indian rhinoceros (*Rhinoceros unicornis*) looks as if it is wearing a suit of armor. On a hot, muggy day in northern India, an Indian rhino wades into a muddy river to cool off. Once common from Pakistan to Myanmar, Indian rhinos are now found only in a few protected parks in India and Nepal.

A few hundred kilometers to the south, in the mountainous rain forests of Sumatra, a small, hairy rhinoceros moves through the dense brush. It stops often to listen.

This Sumatran rhino (*Diceorhinus sumatrensis*), one of the last of its kind, knows that it is in constant danger from large predators such as tigers and human hunters.

South of Sumatra on the island of Java, another rhinoceros pushes through the dense jungle. It is a rare Javan rhinoceros (*Rhinoceros sondaicus*). The Javan rhino once lived throughout Java, Sumatra, and Southeast Asia. Today, the Javan rhinoceros is hardly ever seen. It is the rarest large animal on Earth.

In the early 1800s, more than a million rhinoceroses roamed the plains, forests, and jungles of Africa and Asia. As one of the largest land animals, rhinos were safe from most predators. But about 120 years ago, things changed. The rhino's thick skin was no match for high-powered rifles.

Men with guns hunted rhinos for meat and for **trophies.** Farmers began to burn down forests to plant crops and build cities where the rhinos had once lived. In Yemen, on the Arabian Peninsula, rhino horns were made into dagger handles. Thousands of kilometers away in China, doctors prescribed powdered rhinoceros horn as medicine. More and more rhinos were killed—just for their horns.

In 1970, there were about 65,000 black rhinos in Africa. Today, there are only about 3,600. After a century of hunting, most rhino species are in danger of **extinction.** Most of the survivors live in national parks and preserves, where hunting is illegal.

A group of rhinos grazes in Kruger National Preserve in South Africa.

Chapter Two

A Crash of Rhinos

Rhinoceroses have lived on Earth for about forty million years. Until five million years ago, rhinos were one of the most common large **mammals** in North America, Europe, Africa, and Asia. Dozens of extinct rhino species have been identified from fossils.

Prehistoric rhinos came in all shapes and sizes, from pygmy rhinos less than 1 meter (3 feet) tall to *Indricotherium,* the largest mammal ever to walk the Earth. There were hornless rhinos, five-horned rhinos, and rhinos with two horns side by side.

Wooly rhinos once lived throughout Europe and Asia. Their frozen remains have been found in Siberia. Wooly rhinos were about the same size as the white rhino, but they were covered with a thick coat of hair. Cave paintings in France show the wooly rhino being hunted by prehistoric humans. Wooly rhinos have been extinct since the end of the last ice age, about 10,000 years ago.

Rhinoceroses belong to the mam-

Would You Believe?
The gigantic hornless rhino known as *Indricotherium* lived in Asia about thirty million years ago. It stood about 5.5 meters (18 ft) at the shoulder and weighed more than 10 tons. *Indricotherium*'s long neck helped it reach leaves and fruits growing high in the trees.

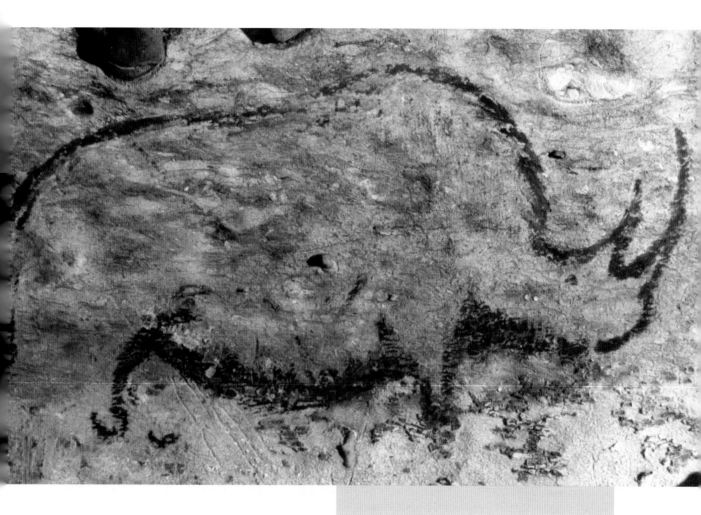

mal group called the perissodactyls. This group of large, plant-eating animals includes rhinos, horses, and tapirs. Perissodactyls are animals that have an odd number of

Cave paintings of woolly rhinos, such as this one found at Rouffignac in southwest France, were made thousands of years ago.

toes. Horses have one toe. Rhinos have three. All perissodactyls' toes end in **hooves.**

Today, only five rhino species remain: the white rhino, the black rhino, the Indian rhino, the Javan rhino, and the Sumatran rhino.

WHITE RHINOS

White rhinos are not really white. They may have gotten their name a long time ago from Europeans who visited Africa and saw that these rhinos were lighter colored than their smaller relatives, the black rhinos. This might have been because the white rhinos had been rolling in light-colored mud or dust. A rhino that is not covered with dust or mud has gray skin.

White rhinos are the largest of the rhinos and the third largest land animal on Earth (elephants and some hippopotamuses are bigger). A full-grown male can weigh 2,500 kilograms (5,500 lbs) and stand 1.8 meters (6 ft) tall at the shoulder. The white rhino has two horns, one on its nose, and the other on its forehead. Its nose horn can grow to more than 1.5 meters (5 ft) long.

White rhinos live on the grassy plains of southern Africa. They have wide mouths that are good for grazing on short grasses. Unlike other rhinoceros species, white

White rhinos aren't really white. Their skin is light gray.

rhinos live in family groups of up to ten animals.

Once common on the grasslands of southern Africa, the white rhino was nearly driven to extinction in the late 1800s. Because the adult rhinos had been safe from predators for millions of years, they had little fear of humans.

A crash of rhinos grazes. White rhinos are the only rhinos that live in family groups.

Hunters with powerful rifles killed them by the thousands for meat, horns, and trophies. By 1900, only about thirty white rhinos were left. Several parks were protected, and hunting white rhinos was outlawed. Their numbers have steadily increased over the last century, and there are now about 11,000 white rhinos living in the wild in South Africa and Zimbabwe.

BLACK RHINOS

Black rhinos are not really black. They are gray. Some people prefer to call them hook-lipped rhinos because they have a hook-shaped, **prehensile** upper lip. The prehensile lip works like a powerful finger or a small trunk—the rhino uses it to grab twigs and leaves.

Black rhinos are slightly smaller than white rhinos, measuring 1.5 meters (5 ft) tall at the shoulder. Adults can weigh up to 1,800 kilograms (4,000 lbs). Like the white rhino, the black rhino has two horns.

Black rhinos are not as sociable as white rhinos. They are seen together only when mating, or when a mother is with its calf. Usually, black rhinos keep to themselves.

In the early 1800s, the black rhinoceros was the most common large animal in Africa. Hundreds of thousands

of black rhinos lived on the grasslands, **savannas,** and shrublands of every African country south of the Sahara desert. Hunting and loss of **habitat** caused the black rhino population to fall rapidly. More than half of the black rhinos had been killed by the end of the nineteenth century.

In 1970, only 70,000 black rhinos were left. Several African countries passed laws against killing rhinos. The laws did not work. **Poachers** continued to hunt rhinos. By 1993, only 2,500 black rhinos remained. They have completely disappeared from Ethiopia, Somalia, Angola, Botswana, Chad, Central African Republic, Malawi, Mozambique, Sudan, and Zambia.

Since then, the people of South Africa, Namibia, Zimbabwe, and Kenya have worked hard to protect their last remaining black rhinos. Over the past decade, the black rhino has increased its numbers to about 3,600.

INDIAN RHINOS

The largest of the Asian rhinoceros species, the Indian rhinoceros is nearly as large as the African white rhino. It usually weighs about 2,200 kilograms (4,840 lbs) and stands close to 1.8 meters (6 ft) tall at the shoulder.

The single nose horn of the Indian rhino is only about 50 centimeters (20 inches) long—not nearly as long as the horns of its African cousins. Its grayish brown skin hangs in thick folds and is covered with bumps. An Indian rhino looks as if it is wearing a suit of impenetrable armor. Like the black rhino, the Indian rhino has a prehensile upper lip.

Indian rhinos once lived throughout Pakistan, northern India, Nepal, and Bangladesh. By 1975, hunting and habitat loss had reduced their numbers to about 600. In recent years, Indian rhino populations have recovered slightly. Today, about 2,400 Indian rhinos live in a few protected parks and **sanctuaries** in northeastern India and Nepal.

Look closely at this rhino. One way to identify it as an Asian rhino is by its thick, bumpy skin that hangs in folds.

Sumatran rhinos are the only rhinos with hair all over their bodies.

JAVAN RHINOS

You are not likely ever to see a Javan rhinoceros. Only about sixty still survive in the tropical forests of Java and Vietnam. There are no Javan rhinos in zoos.

Little is known about Javan rhinos because they are so rare. With folded skin and a single nose horn, the Javan rhino looks like a small version of the Indian rhino—but without the small bumps covering its skin. Female Javan rhinos have a small horn or no horn at all. Javan rhinos weigh about 1,500 kilograms (3,300 lbs) and have prehensile upper lips like their Indian cousins.

SUMATRAN RHINOS

The Sumatran rhino is the smallest of all the rhinoceros species and the only Asian rhino to have two horns. The Sumatran rhino looks very different from its larger cousins. It is quite a bit smaller, standing only 1.2 meters (4 ft) tall at the shoulder. It is also the only rhino to have a coat of hair over its entire body. Only a few hundred Sumatran rhinos are believed to live in the mountainous rain forests of Sumatra, Borneo, and Malaysia.

Chapter Three

From Horn to Tail

What is the first thing you think of when you think of a rhinoceros? Its horn, of course. The name *rhinoceros* comes from the Greek words for "nose" and "horn."

THE DEADLY HORN

The horn of a full-grown African rhino is a fearsome sight. Rhinos use their horns to defend themselves against predators, to push through thick brush, to dig, and to battle other rhinos.

A rhino horn is made of keratin, the same hard, tough substance that makes up fingernails, claws, feathers, and hair. Densely packed strands of keratin grow from patches on the rhino's nose and forehead. The horn keeps on growing throughout the animal's life. African rhinos keep their horns sharp by rubbing them against rocks and tree trunks.

For millions of years, rhinos used their horns to protect themselves. But over the past 200 years, the rhino's horn has brought it to the brink of extinction.

A black rhino has two horns, one on its nose and one on its forehead. While the horns are very useful to the rhino, they also make the animals vulnerable to hunters who kill rhinos for their horns.

The long, sharp horns of African rhinos give them a fierce and unusual appearance. For this reason, rhinos were hunted for trophies during the nineteenth and twentieth centuries. Even though rhino hunting is now outlawed, the slaughter continues in Africa, where rhinos are killed by poachers for their horns. The horns are sold in northern Yemen, where young men are given daggers with handles made from rhino horn as a symbol of adulthood. Rhino horns bring huge prices—a single horn can be sold for several thousand dollars.

Thousands of kilometers away, in India and Southeast Asia, rhinos are also being killed for their horns. In Asia, the horns are not made into daggers. They are ground up and sold as medicine. Powdered rhinoceros horn has been used for many years in traditional Chinese medicine as a fever reducer.

To stop the killing, some conservation groups have tried shooting rhinos with sleep darts, then sawing off their horns. Cutting off a rhino's horns does not hurt the animal—it's like trimming your toenails. The idea was that a hornless rhino would be of no value to a poacher. But rhino horns grow back, and even the stump of a horn is worth a lot of money on the black market. Today, hunters still kill rhinos for their horns.

SKIN AND HAIR

At first glance, the thick skin of a rhinoceros appears to be made of stone or steel. It looks bulletproof, but it's not. Rhino skin is about 2 centimeters (0.75 in) thick. It is tough enough to protect the animal from thorns and sharp twigs, but it can be easily pierced by spears, knives, or bullets. It is also sensitive to touch. Rhinos often wallow in mud or roll in dust to protect their skin from sunburn and biting flies.

A white rhino cow and her calf wallow in the mud in South Africa.

Would You Believe?
The record for the longest horn goes to a male white rhino. His horn was more than 2 meters (6.5 ft) long.

Rhinos are not completely hairless. They have hairs on their ears and at the tip of their tails. Only the Sumatran rhinoceros, which often lives high on cool mountain slopes, has hair all over its body.

SENSES

The rhino's weak eyes are located on the sides of its head. It has to turn its head from side to side to see straight ahead. For the rhino, hearing and smell are its most important senses. Its huge funnel-shaped ears can turn in every direc-

Like all rhinos, this black rhino will have to turn its head to the side to see straight ahead.

tion, and they can pick up sounds that humans can't hear. It uses its sense of smell to identify food plants and other rhinos. As for its sense of taste—who knows? Rhinos will eat almost anything that grows.

FEET AND LEGS

It takes a powerful set of feet to hold up a 2,500-kilogram (5,500-lb) rhinoceros. Each rhino foot has three enormous toes, and each toe ends in a heavy nail, or hoof. Rhinos usually move slowly. But when they have to, their powerful legs can move them at speeds of up to 45 kilometers (30 mi) per hour—faster than the fastest human.

TAIL

When you look at a white rhino's huge 4-meter-long (13-ft-long) body, and then look at its relatively small 64-centimeter-long (25-in-long) tail, you might wonder what purpose the tail serves. But rhinos make use of every part of their bodies. The tail, with its brush of stiff hairs, makes an excellent flyswatter. Rhinos also use their tails to communicate with each other. When a rhino twists its tail into a corkscrew shape, it is saying, "Danger! Look out!"

Would You Believe?
Like its relative the horse, a rhino can sleep lying down or standing up.

Chapter Four

Rhino Behavior

It takes a lot of food to support a rhino-size body. And rhinoceroses love to eat.

DIET

White rhinos spend several hours every morning and evening with their heads hanging low, grazing on grasses. One white rhino can easily eat 20 kilograms (44 lbs) of grass a day. Black rhinos also eat grasses, but they prefer to eat leaves, shoots, and fruit. A black rhino will sometimes stand on its hind legs to reach tender leaves. White and black rhinos have no front teeth. They use their muscular lips to tear off grasses and leaves. They use their **molars** to grind their food before swallowing.

Indian rhinos eat grasses, bamboo, water plants, and leaves. The forest-dwelling Sumatran and Javan rhinos have an unusual feeding technique. They will find a small tree and walk right over it, using the weight of their bodies to bend the tree over until they can reach its fruit and leaves.

GETTING COMFORTABLE

During the heat of the day, African and Indian rhinos rest in the shade or wallow in a pool or mud hole. Indian rhinos are particularly fond of water. They live in swampy areas or along riverbanks where they can wade, swim, and find their favorite foods.

Would You Believe?
Indian and Javan rhinos are the only rhinos that have sharp front teeth, along with a set of large **canine teeth**. These teeth are used for fighting or to defend themselves. Indian and Javan rhinos are also the only rhinos that have one horn instead of two.

An Indian rhino keeps cool in a pool of water.

African rhinos bathe to cool off and wash away biting insects and other **parasites.** If there is no water, a rhino will often roll in the dirt until it is covered with a protective layer of dust.

COMMUNICATION

Like most other mammals, rhinos communicate by using sounds, body language, and smells. A bull rhino will make a growling sound when challenging another bull. Fighting rhinos roar and grunt and squeal. Mother and calf rhinos communicate by whining or mewling. Recently, scientists have learned that rhinos make a sound so low that humans can't hear it. They use this **infrasonic** tone to communicate with each other over long distances.

Scents are an important method of communication for rhinos staking out a territory. All rhinos drop their dung in a well-defined pile that may be scattered afterwards. Bull rhinos spray urine at the borders of their territory to warn others away. Female rhinos use their urine to announce to bull rhinos that it is time to mate.

MATING

Mating rhinos can be a frightening sight. The animals horn wrestle, charge back

Would You Believe?

Oxpeckers are one of the rhino's most important defenses against parasites. These small birds will land on a rhino's back and hop around looking for ticks or insects to eat. Rhinos don't mind the birds—even when they peck inside their ears or nostrils.

and forth, snort, grunt, and squeal. Rhinos often injure each other during these encounters. Once the rhinos have mated, the bull wanders off, and the female goes about her usual business of eating and sleeping. Fifteen to sixteen months later, the female gives birth to a single calf.

Two white rhinos lock horns.

BIG BABIES

Newborn rhino calves weigh 20 to 70 kilograms (44 to 154 lbs), depending on the species. They stand about 0.5 meter (2 ft) tall and look like miniature copies of their parents—except for one thing. The rhino calf has no horn. Instead, it has a smooth, hard plate on its nose. In about a month, the horn will start growing about as fast as a fingernail grows.

A white rhino calf stands next to its mother. If you look carefully, you can see that the baby looks like its mother except it doesn't have a horn yet.

Baby rhinos learn to walk just a few minutes after they are born. The first thing they do once they get to their feet is start nursing. Rhino babies are hungry, so the rhino cow must produce plenty of milk. A mother rhino can produce 20 to 25 liters (5.3 to 6.6 gallons) of milk per day.

Because of the danger from predators, newborn rhino calves stay very close to their mothers. The mother rhino is fierce and aggressive if she thinks her calf is in danger. A group of white rhinos will protect a threatened calf by standing around it in a circle with their horns pointed out.

Rhino calves grow quickly, gaining up to 3 kilograms (6.6 lbs) per day. When they are two or three weeks old, they begin to nibble on leaves and grass. For the next two years, the calf continues to grow on its diet of leaves, grasses, and milk.

By the time it is three years old, a rhino calf has reached its full size and is able to survive without its mother. White rhino calves may stay in the same group with their mothers for many years. Black and Asian rhino mothers drive their calves away when they are about three years old.

By the time a rhino is five years old, it has established its own territory. The young females are ready to have calves of their own. Young male rhinos usually reach maturity

when they are seven to eight years old. Most male rhinos do not mate until they are about ten years old.

Rhinoceroses in zoos can live to be nearly fifty years old. In the wild, rhinos can live to be about thirty-five years old.

This Southern white rhino lives in a zoo. Many zoos have rhinos on exhibit.

Chapter Five

A Future for Rhinos?

As human populations increase, our world is slowly changing. Forests are cut down to make farms. Highways cut through remote wilderness areas. Many species are able to adapt to a loss of habitat. Raccoons have learned to live in sewers and alleys. Crows, pigeons, and sparrows have also taken to city life. Mice and mosquitoes thrive wherever there are people.

Larger animals have a harder time adapting, and rhinoceroses are among the largest of beasts. Rhinos need a lot of room, and they need time to reproduce. A rhino cow has only one calf about every four years, and that calf might not survive its first year. Rhino populations can take a long, long time to recover from threats to their survival.

Most experts believe that both the Sumatran and the Javan rhinoceroses will become extinct during this century. There are simply too few of them left, and they are in constant danger from poachers.

The Indian and African rhinoceroses are also in danger from loss of habitat and illegal hunting. Indian and

Hunters kill many rhinos every year for their horns. This practice has to stop and rhino habitat must be preserved if these animals are going to survive in the wild.

white rhino numbers have increased over the past thirty years, but black rhino numbers continue to decline.

Can the rhinoceroses be saved? Yes! But only if their habitat is preserved and if people stop killing them. Over the past ten years, many more countries have passed laws to protect the last of the rhinos. In Yemen, buying and selling rhino horns is now illegal. Instead, knife makers use plastic or water buffalo horns for dagger handles. In China, modern drugs are replacing rhino horn as a fever remedy.

Who knows? If rhinoceroses are given a chance, they might survive for another 40 million years.

Estimated Rhinoceros Populations (2004)

Black rhino	3,600
Indian rhino	2,400
Javan rhino	60
Sumatran rhino	Fewer than 300
White rhino	11,000

Glossary

canine teeth (KAY-nine TEETH) the large pointed teeth on each side of the jaws of certain animals

dung (DUNG) animal manure

extinction (ek-STINGK-shun) the state of no longer existing

game trails (GAYM TRAYLZ) paths followed by wild animals that are hunted by humans or other predators

graze (GRAYZ) to feed on growing plants

habitat (HAB-uh-tat) the place and conditions in which a plant or an animal lives

hooves (HOOVZ) a hard covering on the feet of certain mammals

infrasonic (in-fruh-SAH-nik) having a sound wave frequency that is below the range of human hearing

mammals (MAM-uhlz) animals that have backbones, have fur or hair, and drink their mother's milk

molars (MOH-lurz) broad, flat teeth used to grind up food

parasites (PA-ruh-sites) animals or plants that get food by living on or in another living thing

poachers (POH-churz) people who hunt animals illegally

predators (PRED-uh-turz) animals that hunt other animals for food

prehensile (pree-HEN-suhl) made for grabbing or gripping by wrapping around an object

sanctuaries (SANGK-choo-ehr-eez) natural areas set aside to shelter and protect animals from hunters

savannas (suh-VAN-uhs) flat, grassy plains

trophies (TRO-feez) game animals that are mounted and hung on walls

For More Information

Watch It

The Rhino War, VHS (Washington, D.C.: National Geographic, 1997).

Read It

Dixon, Franklin W. *The Mystery of the Black Rhino.* New York: Aladdin, 2003.

Murray, Peter. *Rhinos.* Chanhassen, Minn.: The Child's World, 2001.

Nelson, Kristin L. *African Rhinos.* Minneapolis: Lerner Publications, 2005.

Penny, Malcolm. *Black Rhino: Habitats, Life Cycle, Food Chains, Threats.* Austin, Tex.: Raintree Steck-Vaughn, 2001.

Look It Up

Visit our home page for lots of links about rhinos: *http://www.childsworld.com/links*

Note to Parents, Teachers, and Librarians: We routinely verify our Web links to make sure they are safe, active sites—so encourage your readers to check them out!

The Animal Kingdom
Where Do Rhinos Fit In?

Kingdom: Animal

Phylum: Chordates (animals with backbones)

Class: Mammalia (animals that feed their young milk)

Order: Perissodactyla (horses, rhinos, and tapirs)

Family: Rhinocerotidae (rhinoceroses)

Genus and Species:

Ceratotherium simum (white rhino)

Dicerorhinus sumatrensis (Sumatran rhino)

Diceros bicornis (black rhino)

Rhinoceros sondaicus (Javan rhino)

Rhinoceros unicornis (Indian rhino)

Index

About the Author
Peter Murray has written more than 80 children's books on science, nature, history, and other topics. An animal lover, Pete lives in Golden Valley, Minnesota, in a house with one woman, two poodles, several dozen spiders, thousands of microscopic dust mites, and an occasional mouse.